WORLD'S GREATEST COLLECTION OF
OF
Daffy Definitions

Compiled by BOB PHILLIPS

HARVEST HOUSE PUBLISHERS
Eugene, Oregon 97402

**THE WORLD'S GREATEST
COLLECTION OF
DAFFY DEFINITIONS**

Copyright © 1989 by Harvest House Publishers
Eugene, Oregon 97402

Phillips, Bob, 1940-
    The world's greatest collection of daffy definitions;
The world's greatest collection of riddles.

    No collective t.p. Titles transcribed from individual
title pages.
    1. Riddles, Juvenile.   2. Riddles.   I. Phillips,
Bob, 1940- . World's greatest collection of riddles. 1989.
II. Title: World's greatest collection of daffy definitions.
III. Title: World's greatest collection of riddles.
PN6371.5.P49   1989   818'.5402   88-32811
ISBN 0-89081-700-6

Printed in the United States of America.

ABALONE: An expression of disbelief.

ACADEMY AWARDS: A place where everybody lets off esteem.

ACQUAINTANCE: A person you know well enough to borrow money from, but not well enough to lend money to.

ACRIMONY: Another name for marriage.

ACUPUNCTURE: A jab well done.

ADMIRATION: Our polite recognition of another man's resemblance to ourselves.

ADULT: One who has stopped growing, except in the middle.

ADVISORY CAPACITY: The capacity in which a backseat-driver drives.

AIRFLOW: Ventilation of a car created by putting the wife in the backseat.

AIRPLANES: The world's leading cause of white knuckles.

ALARM CLOCK: A frightened timepiece.

ALARM CLOCK: A mechanical device to wake up people who don't have small children.

ALIMONY: Taxation without representation.

ALIMONY: The marital version of "Fly now, pay later."

ALIMONY: Bounty from the mutiny.

ALIMONY: The high cost of leaving.

ALLEGE: A high rock shelf.

ALLEGRO: One leg becoming longer than the other.

AMBITIOUS WIFE: The power behind the drone.

AMISS: Someone who is not married.

AMOUNT: What a soldier in the cavalry rides.

ANNIVERSARIES: When a husband may forget the past, but had better not forget the present.

APOLOGY: Politeness too late.

APPEAL: What a banana comes in.

APPLAUSE: Two hands slapping each other's faces.

ARCHEOLOGICAL TRIP: Bone voyage.

ARCHEOLOGY: A science that proves you can't keep a good man down.

ARREARS: We're supposed to wash behind arrears every day.

ARSON: Our daughter's brother.

ARTISTIC TEMPERAMENT: A disease that afflicts amateurs.

ASCENT: What a hunting dog follows.

ATOLL: What you pay before you cross a bridge.

ATOMIC BOMB: An invention to end all inventions.

AUTHOR: A guy who's usually write.

AUTHORSHIP: A large seagoing vessel belonging to a writer.

AUTOBIOGRAPHY: The life story of an automobile.

AVIATORS: Men who can do anything birds can, except sit comfortably on a barbed wire fence.

BABY: An alimentary canal with a loud voice at one end and no responsibility at the other.

BABY-SITTER: Someone you pay to watch your television and eat your food.

BACHELOR: A man who can be miss-led only so far.

BACHELOR: A fellow who believes it is much better to have loved and lost than to have to get up for the 2 A.M. feeding.

BACHELOR: A man who can take a nap on top of the bedspread.

BACHELOR: A man who prefers to cook his own goose.

BACHELOR: A fellow who doesn't have anyone to share the troubles he doesn't have.

BACHELOR: A man who believes that one can live as cheaply as two.

BACHELOR: A man who never makes the same mistake once.

BACHELOR: Someone who thinks that the only thoroughly justified marriage was the one that produced him.

BACHELOR: One who never Mrs. a girl.

BAD DRIVER: The guy you run into.

BADMINTON: Minton that has been kept in the refrigerator too long.

BAGDAD: What mother did when she met father.

BANK ROBBER: A guy who gets alarmed easily.

BARGAIN HUNTER: One who is often led astray by false profits.

BASKETBALL: A dance held in a basket.

BEASTLY WEATHER: Raining cats and dogs.

BEATNIK: What Nick's father does when Nick is naughty.

BEDROCK: Any rocks you find in your bed.

BEECHNUT: A swim and sun addict.

BEHEAD: What you find at the end of a bee's neck.

BEHOLD: What one bee wrestler uses to pin another bee wrestler.

BELONG: To take your time.

BIG BEN: Tock of the town.

BLIND DATE: When you expect to meet a vision, and she turns out to be a sight.

BLISTER: A heel's revenge for being stepped on.

BOOKKEEPER: A girl who still has the last book you lent her.

BORE: A person who insists upon talking about himself when you want to talk about yourself.

BORE: A person who has nothing to say and says it.

BORE: One who opens his mouth and puts his feats in.

BOREDOM: A state of mind that usually ends when school lets out.

BOSS: The one who is early when you are late and late when you are early.

BOSS: The thing mother allows father to think that he is.

BOY: Like a canoe, he behaves better if paddled from the rear.

BOYCOTT: A bed for a small male child.

BRAT: A child who acts like your own but belongs to someone else.

BREAD: Raw toast.

BRIDAL: A harness for a man.

BRIDEGROOM: The proof that a woman can take a joke.

BRIDEGROOM: A thing they have at a wedding.

BUCK FEVER: Love of money.

BUDGET: A family quarrel.

BULLY: A person with more muscles and less brains than anyone else.

BUMPKIN: To jostle a relative.

BUMPKIN: Your brother, the tramp.

CALENDAR: That which a speaker goes by if he forgets his watch.

CANCER: Cure for smoking.

CAPSIZE: Whatever size cap you take.

CARPET: A dog or cat who enjoys riding in an automobile.

CAR SICKNESS: How you feel each month when the payment is due.

CARTOON: A song sung in an automobile.

CATACOMBS: Instruments for grooming cats.

CAVITY: An empty space waiting to be filled with dentist bills.

CENTURION: A Roman who is a hundred years old.

CHAIRS: Objects that don't move in daytime but at night tiptoe up and kick you in the shins.

CHAIR SHOP: Headquarters for hindquarters.

CHICKEN DINNER: Biting the pullet.

CHICKEN INSPECTOR: A worker who's a cluck watcher.

CHILD: Person who is often spoiled because you can't spank the two grandmothers.

CHILD: A stomach entirely surrounded by curiosity.

CHILDISH GAMES: Those at which your wife beats you.

CHIMNEY SWEEP: Person who does things to soot himself.

CHINESE SPY: A Peking Tom.

CHIROPRACTOR: One who kneads patients.

CHIVALRY: The attitude of a man toward a strange woman.

CHRISTMAS: A holiday on which neither the past nor the future is of as much interest as the present.

CINDER: Large object that looms up just before you wink too late.

CIRCLE: A round straight line with a hole in the middle.

CITY: Millions of people being lonesome together.

CLOSED CORPORATION: Bankruptcy.

COACH: A man who will gladly lay down your life for the team.

COLLECTION: Church function in which many take but a passing interest.

COLLEGE: A mental institution.

COLLEGE BRED: A four-year loaf requiring a fearful amount of dough and seldom self-raising.

COLLEGE CHEER: Money from home.

COMEDIAN: A person with a good memory who hopes other people haven't.

COMMUNITY CHEST: An organization that puts all it begs in one ask it.

COMPLAINT: A grief resumé.

COMPLIMENT: The applause that refreshes.

COMPULSIVE GOLFER: A crackputt.

CONGRESS: Where lawmakers huff and puff and blow up inflation.

COST PLUS: Expensive.

COUNTERFEIT: A seizure while paying your bill at the supermarket.

COURTSHIP: A man pursuing a woman until she catches him.

COWARD: One who, in a perilous emergency, thinks with his legs.

COWARDICE: Yellow, frozen water.

CRITIC: Stowaway on the flight of someone else's imagination.

CRITIC: Legless man who teaches running.

CROOK: A business rival who has just left the room.

CRUMPET: A dog that sits under the table.

CURRENCY: A substance which isn't current enough.

DANDRUFF: Chips off the old block.

DEAD RINGER: A broken telephone.

DEBATE: De fish took debate right off de hook.

DECLARATION OF INDEPENDENCE: A note excusing you from school.

DEJECTION: That condition of mind in which novelists are often found due to the necessity of reading over their work before sending it to the publisher.

DELIVER: Deliver is cooking with de onions.

DENIAL: A river in Egypt.

DERANGE: A place where de cowboys ride.

DERIDED: Thrown from a horse.

DERMATOLOGIST: One who makes rash statements.

DESIRE: The thing that is so often nipped in the budget.

DESK: A trash can with drawers.

DETOUR: The roughest distance between two points.

DIAMOND JUBILEE: When the last installment is paid on the engagement ring.

DICTIONARY: The only place where you'll find success before work.

DIET: The art of letting the hips fall where they sway.

DIET: A short period of starvation preceding a gain of five pounds.

DIETING: Triumph of mind over platter.

DIGNITY: One thing that can't be preserved in alcohol.

DIPLOMACY: The art of convincing a man he's a liar without actually telling him so.

DIPLOMAT: A man who can convince his wife that women look fat in furs.

DIRECTOR: The one who always faces the music.

DIVINE: What da grapes grow on.

DIVORCE: Hash made of domestic scraps.

DIVORCE: When one man's mate is another man's poison.

DIVOT: A piece of dead turf found on a golf ccurse.

DOCTOR: A man who suffers from good health.

DOGMA: A mother dog.

DOGMATIC: A kind of revolver carried by police dogs.

DOG POUND: A used cur lot.

DOG SLED: Polar coaster.

DOLLAR: The jack of all trades.

DOLLAR SIGN: An S that's been double crossed.

DON RICKLES: The Merchant of Menace.

DRAFTSMAN: A husband who leaves windows open.

DRAMATIC CRITIC: One who gives the best jeers of his life to the theater.

DREAMER: One who waits for something to turn up—a doer turns up something while waiting.

DRINKING: An act which does not drown your sorrows, it only irrigates them.

DRIVER: One who horns in.

DRUM: An instrument you can't beat for noise.

DUCKBILL: A demand for payment of any ducks you bought.

DUTIES: Tasks we look forward to with distaste, perform with reluctance, and brag about ever after.

EARTHQUAKE: A topographical error.

ECCENTRIC: An Oddfellow.

ECONOMY: Way of spending money without getting any fun out of it.

EGOTIST: Someone who is always me-deep in conversation.

ELECTROCARDIOGRAPH: A ticker tape.

ELLIPTICAL: The feel of a kiss.

ENGAGEMENT RING: A tourniquet applied to the third finger of a girl's left hand to stop circulation.

ETC: Sign used to make others believe you know more than you do.

EUREKA: A euphemism for "You smell bad."

EXERCISE: Droop therapy.

EXPERIENCED MARRIED MAN: One who can tell when he and his wife come to the end of one argument and begin another.

EXPLORER: A guy who gets enough facts for a book.

FALSEHOOD: Somone who pretends to be a gangster.

FAT MEN: Usually good-natured because it takes them so long to get mad clear through.

FENCER: A guy who puts up fences.

FERN: A plant that you're supposed to water once a day, but when you don't it dies; but if you do, it dies anyway, only not so soon.

FIGHT ARENA: A punch bowl.

FILING CABINET: A metal box where you can systematically lose things.

FINITE: A beautiful evening.

FINLAND: A place where a lot of sharks live.

FIREPROOF: The boss' relatives.

FIREWOOD: Chopped sticks.

FLABBERGASTED: The state you get in when you're overwhelmed by a flabber.

FLASHLIGHT: A case to carry dead batteries in.

FLATTERY: Soft soap, and soft soap is 90 percent lye.

FLATTERY: Phony express.

FLIRT: The girl who got the boy you wanted.

FLIRT: A hit-and-run lover.

FLIRTING: The gentle art of making a man feel pleased with himself.

FLOOD: A river too big for its bridges.

FLORIST: A petal pusher.

FODDER: The man who married Mudder.

FOOTLIGHT: A light used by doctors for examining people's toes.

FORGER: A man who makes a name for himself.

FRAU: Many a man lives by the sweat of his frau.

FREEDOM: Being able to do what you please without considering anyone except the wife; police; boss; life insurance company; state, federal and city authorities; and the neighbors.

FREETHINKER: A bachelor.

FRIGHTENED FLOWER ARRANGER: A petrified florist.

FRUSTRATION: Buying a new boomerang and finding it impossible to throw the old one away.

FUR COATS: Not to keep women warm but to keep them quiet. Sheep at any price.

FUTILE REMARK: The one a man makes for the purpose of changing the subject when the wife complains because he has forgotten their wedding anniversary or her birthday.

GARDEN: Place where some of the bulbs seem to think they're buried instead of planted.

GARGOYLE: Something you wash your throat with when it's sore.

GIRDLE MANUFACTURER: Another fellow who lives off the fat of the land.

GOBLET: A baby turkey.

GOLF: Game where most of us stand too close to the ball—after we have hit it.

GOLF: A game which improves your health and enables you to understand the jokes in the comic section of the newspaper.

GOSSIP: Good memory with a tongue hung in the middle of it.

GRUESOME: A little taller than before.

GUILLOTINE: Something that will give a person a pain in the neck.

GUMDROP: A receptacle for used chewing gum.

HABIT: That which makes father, after working his way through college, work his son's way through.

HALF-WIT: Person who spends half his time thinking up wisecracks and definitions.

HANDSOME: A term useful in requesting things, as in, "Handsome more chicken to me."

HANGOVER: What you get if you eat too much.

HAPPINESS: Perfume you cannot pour on others without getting a few drops on yourself.

HAPPY MARRIAGE: A long conversation that always seems too short.

HARI-KARI: Transporting a wig from one place to another.

HARP: A nude piano.

HATE: The benevolent feeling which California has for Florida and vice versa.

HENPECKED HUSBAND: One who gives his wife the best ears of his life.

HIGHBORN: Anybody born on top of a mountain.

HIGH HEELS: The invention of a girl who had been kissed on the forehead too many times.

HIGH-MINDED: Anybody whose head comes to a point.

HIJACK: A jack for changing tires on airplanes.

HOLLYWOOD MARRIAGE: A rest period between romances.

HOME: Place where you don't have to engage reservations in advance.

HOME PLATE: A dish found in the home.

HONEYMOON: The vacation a man takes before beginning work under a new boss.

HORSE DOCTOR: Any horse that graduated from medical school.

HORSE SENSE: Stable thinking.

HORSE SENSE: What makes horses never bet on people.

HOSPITALS: Places where people who are run-down wind up.

HOUSEWARMING: Last call for wedding presents.

HOWLING SUCCESS: The baby that always gets picked up.

HUG: A roundabout way of expressing your love.

HUMDINGER: A person who hums while ringing a bell.

HUMORIST: A writer who shows us the faults of human nature in such a way that we recognize our failings and smile—and our neighbor's and laugh.

HUNGER: What the posse did to the lady rustler.

HUSBAND: A man for whom the bills toll.

HUSBAND: A man of few words.

HUSBAND: A man who's like an egg—if kept continually in hot water he becomes hard-boiled.

HYPOCRITICAL: Anyone who tells you your hips are getting too big.

HYPODERMIC NEEDLE: A sick-shooter.

ICEBERG: A kind of permanent wave.

IDEAL: My turn to shuffle.

IDEALS: Funny little things that don't work unless you do.

ILLEGAL: A sick bird.

INSANITY: Grounds for divorce in some states; grounds for marriage in all.

INSPIRED: Having sat on a steeple.

INTELLIGENCE: A sterling quality possessed by anybody who will listen attentively to what you have to say and nod in agreement.

INTENSE: Where campers sleep.

INTERNATIONAL CONSCIENCE: The still small voice that tells a country when another country is stronger.

IRON ORE: An oar you can hardly row with.

JANITOR: A floor flusher.

JOINT CHECKING ACCOUNT: A device that permits the wife to beat you to the draw.

JOKE: What some people tell and others marry.

JOY OF MOTHERHOOD: What a woman experiences when all the kids are in bed.

JUMP: The last word in airplanes.

JUNE: When young men graduate from college and begin their education.

JUNK: Something you keep ten years and then throw away two weeks before you need it.

JUNKYARD: Hong Kong harbor on a busy day.

KAZOO: The sound of a sneeze.

KIBITZER: A person with an interferiority complex.

KINGDOM: A king who isn't very bright.

KINSHIP: Your rich uncle's boat.

KNAPSACK: A sleeping bag.

LADY-IN-WAITING: The feminine of bachelor.

LADY PILOT: A plane Jane.

LAPLANDER: Someone who jumps onto other people's laps.

LAUGH: A smile that burst.

LAUNDRESS: A gown worn while sitting on the grass.

LAWSUIT: A policeman's uniform.

LEMONADE: A government program to assist underprivileged lemons.

LIBERTY: What a man exchanges for a wife.

LIFE INSURANCE: The thing that keeps you poor all your life so you can die rich.

LIMERICK: A witty ditty.

LIPSTICK: Something which merely adds color and flavor to an old pastime.

LITTLE LEAGUER: Peanut batter.

LOBOTOMY: Short-leggedness.

LOCOMOTIVE: A ridiculous reason for doing something.

LOVE: The softening of the hearteries.

LOVE: An island of emotion entirely surrounded by expenses.

LOVE: Perpetual emotion.

LOVE: A heart attack.

LOVE: A heartburn.

LOVE: The only fire against which there is no insurance.

MAGICIAN: A super duper.

MAGICIAN: Anyone nowadays who can make the weekly paycheck last a week.

MAGPIE: A pie baked by a woman named Maggie.

MALE: The only thing you can't get from a mail-order house.

MAP: Something that will tell you everything except how to fold it up again.

MARRIAGE: Declaration of War.

MARRIED MAN: One who has two hands with which to steer a car.

MARRIED MAN: A guy who always turns off the motor when his wife calls, "I'll be right out."

MARS: The red barren.

MATRIMONY: The only union which permits a woman to work unlimited overtime without extra pay.

MELANCHOLIC: Indigestion in watermelon time.

MEMBRANE: The part of your brain you remember with.

MENU: A list of dishes the restaurant has just run out of.

METRIC COOKIE: A gram cracker.

MINOR OPERATION: One performed on somebody else.

MISCHIEF: The chief's daughter.

MISER: A dough nut.

MISJUDGE: A lady judge who's not married.

MODEL HUSBAND: Always some other woman's.

MODERN EDUCATION: Learning the three R's— rah, rah, rah!

MONOLOGUE: A conversation being carried on by a man and his wife.

MOTHER-IN-LAW: A woman who is never outspoken.

MUGWUMP: One who sits on a political fence with his mug on one side and his wump on the other.

NAG: A woman with no horse sense.

NAGGING: The constant reiteration of the unhappy truth.

NARROW-MINDED: Taking a size 2 hat.

NATURAL SELECTION: To take the largest piece.

NECESSITY: Almost any luxury you see in the home of a neighbor.

NET INCOME: The money a fisherman earns.

NEXT WAR: War which will be fought with radio waves and no doubt everyone will be bored to death.

NITRATE: Cheapest price for calling long-distance.

OBESITY: Surplus gone to waist.

OBSCURITY: Being the vice-president of Italy.

OCTOPUS: A cat with only eight lives left.

OIL: Wealth that slips through your fingers.

OLD MAID: A lady in waiting.

OLD MAID: A lady in waiting and waiting and waiting.

ONE-LINER: A mini ha-ha.

OPERETTA: A girl who works for the telephone company.

OPPORTUNIST: Any man who goes ahead and does what you always intended to do.

OPTIMIST: A person who thinks humorists will eventually run out of definitions of an optimist.

OPTIMIST: He who thinks a housefly is looking for the way out.

ORATOR: One who misses many fine opportunities for keeping quiet.

OUTLYING: Gone to court.

OVEREATING: The destiny that shapes our ends.

OVEREATING: An activity that will make you thick to your stomach.

PANAMA CANAL: An inside strait.

PARADISE: Two ivory cubes with dots all over them.

PARALYZE: Two untruths.

PARKING SPACE: Unoccupied space on the other side of the street.

PASSPORT PHOTO: Way to see yourself as others see you.

PEANUT BUTTER: A bread spread.

PEASHOOTER: A baby blowgun.

PEDESTRIAN: A father who has kids who can drive.

PEDIATRICIAN: A man with little patients.

PEEKABOO: The act of spying on a ghost.

PESSIMIST: An optimist on his way home from Las Vegas.

PESSIMIST: One who thinks he is taking a chance—the optimist thinks he is grasping an opportunity.

PHILOSOPHY: Unintelligible answers to insoluble problems.

PHOTOGRAPH ALBUMS: The strange views people take of things.

PHRENOLOGY: The science of picking the pocket through the scalp.

PICKPOCKET: Someone who never learned to keep his hands to himself.

PIG IRON: An iron for smoothing wrinkles off pigs.

PINE TREE: A tree that mopes.

PNEUMONIA: What you get after you've had old monia.

POISE: The ability to continue talking while the other fellow picks up the check.

POLICE HELICOPTER: The whirlybird that catches the worm.

POLITICIAN: One whose greatest asset is his lie-ability.

POOL CUE: A line of people waiting to go swimming.

POPOVER: The thing that happens when you put too much corn in the corn popper.

POSITIVE: Being mistaken at the top of one's voice.

POST OFFICE: U.S. Snail.

POT HOLDER: A corset.

POVERTY: State of mind sometimes induced by a neighbor's new car.

PRACTICAL JOKES: Pranks for the memory.

PRAISE: Letting off esteem.

PRECINCT: Sunk before you could get there.

PROFESSIONAL HUMORIST: One who has a good memory and hopes others haven't.

PROPOSAL: An attempt to acquire a huge vocabulary.

PROSPERITY: The sweet buy and buy.

PSYCHIATRIST: A person who beats a psychopath to your door.

PUPPY LOVE: The beginning of a dog's life.

PUP TENT: A canvas doghouse.

QUACK: A doctor who ducks the law.

QUADRUPLETS: Four crying out loud.

RAMPAGE: The page in the encyclopedia about male sheep.

RAMPART: Paintings displayed on a ramp.

RATTAN: What a rat gets while vacationing in Florida.

RAZOR BLADE THEME SONG: "Nobody Knows the Stubble I've Seen."

RECKLESS DRIVER: One who is seldom wreckless for long.

REDSKINS: People on the American bathing beaches.

REMARRIAGE: The triumph of hope over experience.

RENO: A large inland seaport in America with the tide running in and the untied running out.

RENO: Where the honeymoon express is finally uncoupled.

REPARTEE: An insult with a college education.

RESTAURANT: An institution for the distribution of indigestion.

RESTITUTION: A home for chronically exhausted people.

RHUBARB: Bloodshot celery.

RICE: A product associated with the worst mistake of some men's lives.

ROCK BOTTOM: A rocking chair.

RUBBER TREES: Stretch plants.

SALARY: Enough money to cover carfare and lunch for a week.

SALESMAN: A man who convinces his wife she looks fat in a mink coat.

SALES RESISTANCE: The triumph of mind over platter.

SANTA CLAUS: Person who does not come through the chimney but through a large hole in the pocketbook.

SARCASM: Quip lash.

SCREEN DOOR: What kids get a bang out of.

SCREENS: An invention for keeping flies in the house.

SECRET: Something that is either not worth keeping, or too good to keep.

SECRET: Something that is hushed about from place to place.

SENSE OF HUMOR: What makes you laugh at something which would make you mad if it happened to you.

SENSE OF HUMOR: Being able to laugh at your friend's misfortunes.

SHOPLIFTER: A person with a gift of grab.

SHORTCUT: A trim at the barbershop.

SHOTGUN WEDDING: A case of wife or death.

SIC: Not feeling well.

SILENCE: The only successful substitute for brains.

SINCERE FRIEND: One who says nasty things to your face, instead of saying them behind your back.

SLOWPOKE: The punch a tired boxer throws.

SMART MAN: One who keeps his eyes wide open before marriage and half-shut afterward.

SNORING: A form of sheet music.

SNORING: A pleasure that is all yours.

SOOTHSAYING: Comforting.

SOUND THINKER: One whose opinions coincide with our own.

SOUTHPAW: A baseball player from below the Mason-Dixon line.

SPANKING: Stern punishment.

SPINSTER: The most singular of women.

SPINSTER: A woman who goes around and around looking for a man.

SPINSTER: A woman who is unhappily unmarried.

SPINSTER: Lady in waiting.

SPIRITUALIST: A trance-guesser.

SPRING: Time of year when a young man's fancy turns to what the girls have been thinking about all winter.

STALEMATE: A wife who is beginning to smell musty.

STATIONERY STORE: A store that stays pretty much at the same location.

STIRRUP: What you do with cake batter.

STORK: The bird with the big bill.

STRIKING SERMON: One which hits the man who is not there.

STUCCO: What you get when you sit on gummo.

STUPENDOUS: Advance stupidity.

SUBSIDY: A town underneath another town.

SUGAR DADDY: One form of crystallized sap.

SURFER: Man-over-board.

SURREY MAKERS: People who are always looking for fringe benefits.

SUSPICIOUS CHARACTER: A man who suspects everybody.

SWEATER: A garment worn by a small child when his mother feels chilly.

SWIMMING POOL: A crowd of people with water in it.

SYNONYM: A word used when you can't spell the word you want.

SYNTAX: A new tax that should bring in all the money the government needs.

TACT: What you don't say when you're angry.

TACT: What you think but don't say.

TAILOR SHOP: Last of the big-time menders.

TAXES: A place with a lot of cowboys.

TAXIDERMIST: Man who knows his stuff.

TAXPAYERS: People who don't have to take a civil service test to work for the government.

TEARS: The world's greatest waterpower.

TELEPATHY: A disease that you get from talking on the phone too much.

TEMPERAMENTAL: Ninety percent temper; ten percent mental.

TENURE: The number following nineure.

TEXT: That which ministers preach from, and often vary far from.

THIEF: A person who has the habit of finding things before the owner loses them.

THUMB: A modern means of transportation.

TIME: The shortest known unit is the time between the change of the traffic light and the honk from the boob behind you.

TOLERANCE: The art of putting up with people who aren't perfect like you.

TRAFFIC JAM: A substance for spreading on streets at five o'clock.

TRAFFIC LIGHT: A little green light that changes to red as your car approaches.

TRAPEZE ARTIST: A guy who gets the hang of things.

TRICYCLE: A tot rod.

TREE: Something that will stand in the same place for 60 years and then suddenly jump in front of a car.

TROJAN HORSE: A phony pony.

TULIPS: The standard number of lips assigned to each person.

TURTLE: A reptile who lives in a mobile home.

TWINS: Infant replay.

UNABATED: A mousetrap without any cheese or a fishhook without a worm.

UNABRIDGED: A river you have to wade across.

UNCLE SAM: The one who wears a tall hat so he can pass it around.

UNISON: An only male child.

UNTOLD WEALTH: That which does not appear on the income tax returns.

UNTOUCHABLES: People as broke as we are.

VALUABLE SENSE OF HUMOR: One that enables a person to see instantly what isn't safe to laugh at.

VANGUARD: A person who protects trucks.

VENTRILOQUIST: A person who talks to himself for a living.

VICIOUS CIRCLE: Bad company.

VIOLIN: An instrument for musicians who like to fiddle around.

VISION: What people think you have when you guess correctly.

WALKIE-TALKIE: The opposite of sittie-stillie.

WAVELENGTH: The distance from the scalp to the end of a curl.

WEATHER: That about which the most is said and the least done.

WEDDING RING: A one-man band.

WILL: A dead giveaway.

WINDJAMMER: A person who spreads jelly on bread during a hurricane.

WINDOW-SHOPPER: A store gazer.

WOMAN: Creature whom God made beautiful that man might love her, and unreasonable that she might love man.

WOMEN'S LIB: A Ms. is as good as a male.

WORK: An unpopular way of earning money.

WORLD: A big ball that revolves on its taxes.

WORLD'S BEST AFTER-DINNER SPEECH: "Waiter, give me both checks."

WORRY: Interest paid on trouble before it falls due.

WRINKLE-PROOF: An affidavit stating that you have wrinkles.

WRITER'S CRAMP: Authoritis.

X-RAY: Belly vision.

YAWN: Nature's way of letting a husband open his mouth.

YAWN: A silence with an exclamation mark.

YAWN: A silent shout.

YES-MAN: Someone who is married.

ZINC: What will happen to you if you don't know how to zwim.

ZOO: A place where animals look at silly people.

More
Harvest House Books
by Bob Phillips

THE ALL AMERICAN JOKE BOOK

A riotous, fun-filled collection of over 800 anecdotes, puns, and jokes.

BIBLE FUN

Jam-packed full of brain-teasing crossword puzzles, intricate mazes, word jumbles, and other mind benders. *Bible Fun* will keep you occupied for hours—with the added bonus of honing your Bible knowledge. Sharpen your pencil and put your thinking cap on—you're about to be a-maze-d!

THE LAST OF THE GOOD CLEAN JOKES

The master joker edits and arranges wisecracks, rib ticklers, and zany puns.

MORE GOOD CLEAN JOKES

An entertaining fun-book designed for public speakers, pastors, and everyone who enjoys good clean jokes.

THE RETURN OF THE GOOD CLEAN JOKES

Over 900 quips, anecdotes, gags, puns, and wisecracks.

Other Good Harvest House Books

PROVERBS FOR PEOPLE
by Vern McClellan

Clever, provocative proverbs are matched with a corresponding Bible reference and illustration that will bring a smile and a cause for reflection with the turn of each page. Here's a sample: Proverb: He who gossips usually winds up in his own mouthtrap. Proverbs 16:28: An evil man sows strife; gossip separates the best of friends.

QUIPS, QUOTES, AND QUESTS
by Vern McClellan

You'll never be without a wise or witty saying after you read *Quips, Quotes, and Quests*. This inspiring collection of 1,098 famous (and infamous) quotations, Bible verses, and common sense sayings is a handy reference book for the whole family. If you like stimulating, insightful one-liners, this is the book for you.

PROVERBS, PROMISES, AND PRINCIPLES
by Vern McClellan

This inspiring book is jammed with penetrating insights and poignant points that will add exciting new dimensions to your life and conversation. If you're a teacher, preacher, writer, researcher, parent or student, you'll find humorous, practical proverbs, timely Bible promises, and powerful principles to apply to living.

Dear Reader:

We would appreciate hearing from you regarding this Harvest House nonfiction book. It will enable us to continue to give you the best in Christian publishing.

1. What most influenced you to purchase *The World's Greatest Collection of Daffy Definitions/Riddles?*
   - ☐ Author
   - ☐ Subject matter
   - ☐ Backcover copy
   - ☐ Recommendations
   - ☐ Cover/Title
   - ☐ _____

2. Where did you purchase this book?
   - ☐ Christian bookstore
   - ☐ General bookstore
   - ☐ Other
   - ☐ Grocery store
   - ☐ Department store

3. Your overall rating of this book:
   - ☐ Excellent
   - ☐ Very good
   - ☐ Good
   - ☐ Fair
   - ☐ Poor

4. How likely would you be to purchase other books by this author?
   - ☐ Very likely
   - ☐ Somewhat likely
   - ☐ Not very likely
   - ☐ Not at all

5. What types of books most interest you?
   (check all that apply)
   - ☐ Women's Books
   - ☐ Marriage Books
   - ☐ Current Issues
   - ☐ Self Help/Psychology
   - ☐ Bible Studies
   - ☐ Fiction
   - ☐ Biographies
   - ☐ Children's Books
   - ☐ Youth Books
   - ☐ Other _____

6. Please check the box next to your age group.
   - ☐ Under 18
   - ☐ 18-24
   - ☐ 25-34
   - ☐ 35-44
   - ☐ 45-54
   - ☐ 55 and over

Mail to: Editorial Director
Harvest House Publishers
1075 Arrowsmith
Eugene, OR 97402

Name _____

Address _____

City _____ State _____ Zip _____

Dear Reader:

We would appreciate hearing from you regarding this Harvest House nonfiction book. It will enable us to continue to give you the best in Christian publishing.

1. What most influenced you to purchase *The World's Greatest Collection of Daffy Definitions/Riddles?*
   - [ ] Author
   - [ ] Recommendations
   - [ ] Subject matter
   - [ ] Cover/Title
   - [ ] Backcover copy

2. Where did you purchase this book?
   - [ ] Christian bookstore
   - [ ] Grocery store
   - [ ] General bookstore
   - [ ] Department store
   - [ ] Other

3. Your overall rating of this book:
   - [ ] Excellent [ ] Very good [ ] Good [ ] Fair [ ] Poor

4. How likely would you be to purchase other books by this author?
   - [ ] Very likely
   - [ ] Not very likely
   - [ ] Somewhat likely
   - [ ] Not at all

5. What types of books most interest you? (check all that apply)
   - [ ] Women's Books
   - [ ] Fiction
   - [ ] Marriage Books
   - [ ] Biographies
   - [ ] Current Issues
   - [ ] Children's Books
   - [ ] Self Help/Psychology
   - [ ] Youth Books
   - [ ] Bible Studies
   - [ ] Other _____

6. Please check the box next to your age group.
   - [ ] Under 18 [ ] 25-34 [ ] 45-54
   - [ ] 18-24 [ ] 35-44 [ ] 55 and over

Mail to: Editorial Director
Harvest House Publishers
1075 Arrowsmith
Eugene, OR 97402

Name _____

Address _____

City _____ State _____ Zip _____